DOUBLE CHEESEBURGERS, Quiche, and Vegetarian Burritos

AMERICAN COOKING FROM THE 1920S THROUGH TODAY

By
Loretta Frances Ichord

Illustrated by
Jan Davey Ellis

M MILLBROOK PRESS ◆ MINNEAPOLIS

For my wonderful editor, Jean E. Reynolds,
who opened that first door

I would like to thank the interesting and informative guides at COPIA: The American Center for Wine, Food, and the Arts. I also want to thank Chez Panisse for its excellent service and food. And lastly, I would like to give a cheer for all the hardworking farmers who get up early to pick their dew-covered produce to sell at farmers' markets across the United States.

Contents

Introduction

If you were a hungry time traveler who had landed in the United States during the 1920s, what would you find to eat? Would you find a Taco Bell and order four tacos to go? Or maybe you'd locate a sushi bar and eat raw fish? But neither of these eating establishments would have been around in the early twentieth-century United States. Many Americans at that time had little knowledge of Mexican food or Japanese prepared rice and raw fish dishes. Early twentieth-century Americans could not have imagined how much culinary tastes would change and evolve in the next one hundred years.

Though the history of American eating began when the first colonists arrived in the New World in the seventeenth century, the most dramatic changes in the way Americans cook and eat occurred in the twentieth century. No other century saw a woman's role in the kitchen make such sweeping changes from backbreaking drudgery to easy meal preparation because of the advances in kitchen appliances and cooking gadgets. Plus during the last century, new food products, dining habits, food magazines, cookbooks, chefs as famous as movie stars, and many world events all had an impact on the American homemaker and the way we eat in the twenty-first century.

This book will cover eating habits in the United States from 1920 up to the present time in the twenty-first century. Eight recipes, which span the changing tastes in the United States, are included in the text with notes explaining how and when each dish became popular. You can prepare these foods with the help of an adult in your home or at school with your teacher and classmates. An appendix in the back of the book will tell you how to increase the ingredients for classroom projects.

So enjoy the flavors of the past, present, and future!

American Cooking and Eating in the Mid-Twentieth Century:

1920–1959

Putting Three Square Meals on the Table

In the beginning of the twentieth century, it was still a time-consuming task to cook three square meals a day. (This term came from colonial times when food was eaten from a square, hollowed-out block of wood called a trencher.) Though these meals were no longer cooked in a large fireplace, many women in the early 1900s spent an average of forty-four hours a week in the kitchen, preparing meals and cleaning up after them. Food was cooked on a coal- or wood-burning stove that was difficult to use and very messy to clean because of the soot it created. Many women in the upper middle class or upper class had servants who did most of this drudgery, but not-so-wealthy women were stuck with these cooking chores, plus cleaning the rest of the home, doing laundry, and taking care of children. But soon things were about to change in the everyday life of the American housewife.

By the 1920s, improvements in the American kitchen were being felt by many urban households. Electric and gas lines were becoming more and

more available in private homes (rural areas were slower in getting these lines). Indoor plumbing had also made its entrance. New laborsaving appliances, such as gas or electric stoves, refrigerators, electric mixers, toasters, utensils, special pots and pans, and processed foods all cut down on the hours spent in the kitchen. These features were welcomed by the middle class as well because servants in private homes were leaving to work in factories and other better-paying positions.

Here is a list of a few of the many processed foods developed in the 1920s and 1930s. You may be surprised to see how long these familiar foods have been around.

WONDER BREAD (1921) ♦ The Taggart Baking Company of Indianapolis, Indiana, came out with a one and a half pound loaf of white bread that contained preservatives to keep it fresh. In 1930 WONDER BREAD was sold as sliced bread (Otto Frederick Rohwedder invented the first machine that sliced and wrapped bread in 1928). From this new product came the expression, "The greatest thing since sliced bread."

QUAKER OATS (1921) ♦ The Quaker Oats Company introduced quick-cooking oatmeal (cooked in five minutes instead of twenty), and it became one of the United States' first convenience foods.

WHEATIES (1924) ♦ The Washburn-Crosby Company introduced this cereal that would become known as the Breakfast of Champions.

PETER PAN PEANUT BUTTER (1928) ♦ Swift Packing Company introduced its first hydrogenated (chemical process that makes unsaturated fat more solid), homogenized peanut butter (the homogenization process of keeping the peanut butter from separating) invented by J. L. Rosefield in 1922. In 1932 Rosefield produced his own brand and called it SKIPPY PEANUT BUTTER.

RICE KRISPIES (1928) ♦ This cereal, one of many by the Kellogg Company, had the popular saying, "Snap! Crackle! Pop!" first appear on its box in 1932. The three happy gnomes came along in 1933 to represent the sounds of the food. In Sweden these characters say, "Piff! Paff! Puff!" and in Germany they say, "Knisper! Knasper! Knusper!"

GERBER BABY FOOD (1929) ♦ Daniel Gerber began selling strained baby foods in cans to grocery stores. Some mothers resisted buying the product until salt was added to it in 1931. Babies couldn't tell the difference, but mothers who tasted their babies' food could.

BIRDS EYE FROSTED FOODS (1930) ♦ General Foods introduced Birds Eye Frosted Food. They were advertised as foods fresh frozen that traveled from plant to store to rental freezer (the only freezers available before home freezers were developed). These frosted foods were developed by Clarence Birdseye (father of the frozen-food industry) when he discovered during a visit to the Arctic in 1914 that fish pulled from icy waters froze rock hard and could be kept for weeks. When they were cooked, they tasted fresh. However, the system of buying and keeping frozen foods had some drawbacks for the consumer. In the 1930s and 1940s, people had to rent a space at a frozen-food locker plant to store their frosted food. When they wanted to use frozen food, they had to drive to the locker, making the system inconvenient until home freezers arrived in the 1950s.

FRITOS CORN CHIPS (1932) ♦ Ice-cream salesman Elmer Doolin ate lunch in a Texas sandwich shop that was selling fried corn chips (made with Mexican corn masa). He bought the recipe, the FRITOS name, and a potato ricer for one hundred dollars from Gustave Olguin, the owner of the shop. Doolin kept expanding his territory to sell FRITOS corn chips until he eventually merged his company in 1961 with the H. W. Lay Company, and the name Frito-Lay, Inc., was created. Soon many Americans loved to "muncha buncha Fritos."

RITZ CRACKERS (1933) ♦ The National Biscuit Company developed a round, buttery cracker and called it Ritz because it was so rich tasting.

KRAFT MACARONI & CHEESE DINNER (1937) ♦ Kraft Macaroni & Cheese Dinner was introduced by National Dairy Products and consisted of grated American cheese and Tenderoni Macaroni in a box. It was advertised on the Kraft Music Hall radio show as "a meal for four in nine minutes for an everyday price of nineteen cents."

SPAM & COMPANY (1937) ♦ This spiced ham product, introduced by the George A. Hormel Company, would become the world's largest-selling canned meat by 1942 when the United States entered World War II.

Millions of cans of this fatty ground pork shoulder mixed with salt, ham, sugar, and sodium nitrite were shipped overseas to feed the Allied troops.

NESTLÉ CORPORATION'S CHOCOLATE MORSELS (1939) ♦ Nestlé developed chocolate morsels (chocolate chips) to go in Toll House cookies. In 1930 Ruth Wakefield invented the actual recipe for chocolate chip cookies in her Toll House Inn in Whitman, Massachusetts. It happened by accident when Wakefield was making cookies for her customers, and she realized that she was out of baker's chocolate. In a panic, she chopped up a semisweet chocolate bar and dumped the pieces into the cookie dough. After baking the cookies, she was surprised to see that the chocolate didn't melt into the dough as she had expected, and the United States' favorite cookie, the chocolate chip, was born. In 1939 she signed a contract with Nestlé to let them use her Toll House recipe on the back of their morsel packages.

Though the advances in kitchen appliances and processed foods eased the American woman's work in the kitchen and gave her more free time, she was still responsible for putting three square meals on the table for her family. Knowing how to cook was a necessary skill for all homemakers, even wealthy women who had lost their kitchen servants. To educate these women, a prim and proper woman by the name of Fannie Farmer (1857–1915) appeared on the scene with her precise instructions on how to measure and combine ingredients in recipes.

Fannie Farmer was a teacher and later a principal of the Boston Cooking School when she became nationally known for her cookbook *The Boston Cooking-School Cook Book* published in 1896. Farmer approached recipes in a scientific manner by doing away with old-fashioned and vague directions used in the past such as measuring out a peck of flour or a lump of dough, adding lard the size of a hen's egg, putting in a piece of butter as big as a walnut, or using a ladleful of batter. She wrote in her book: "Correct measurements are absolutely necessary to insure the best results." She instructed cooks to measure ingredients by level cups and spoonfuls. She became known as the Mother of Level Measurement.

Even after Fannie Farmer's death in 1915, her book was so popular that it went through many updated and revised editions in the twentieth century by her niece, Wilma Lord Perkins. Eventually, the newer editions were simply titled *The Fannie Farmer Cookbook*. In the 1970s, a cookbook author, Marian Cunningham, completely overhauled Farmer's recipes to suit more modern tastes.

With Fannie Farmer's book providing help in the kitchen, new food products, and newly purchased appliances, the 1920s was a decade of prosperity.

Yes, life was looking good until October 29, 1929, blasted away the good times. On this day, forever known as Black Tuesday, the United States was thrown into the most desperate of financial disasters.

THE GREAT DEPRESSION ♦ When the stock market crashed in 1929, many banks and businesses closed their doors, leaving thousands of people without jobs and money. All of a sudden, Americans were forced to make due with less. They had to learn to use every scrap of food they could get in order to stretch meals for their families. Many city people waited in long lines for bread or soup. Some existed on cheap hot dogs or hamburgers purchased from automats (vending machines in cafeterias). Farmers struggled with the low prices for their crops and bad weather. Many lost their farms.

Americans survived during these hard times in some of the following ways: Many families moved in with other families. The bartering system became very popular when food was traded for any kind of service or work. Restaurants, organizations, and private citizens dumped food for the taking in big open spaces called free food dumps for the poor and homeless. States, relief agencies, universities, and corporations started group gardens.

Then in 1933, President Franklin Delano Roosevelt started a program called the New Deal, which created dozens of agencies that protected bank depositors, regulated the Stock Exchange, began working on a social security system, and formed the Work Projects Administration (WPA) to create jobs.

While all this was going on, women became very creative in trying to put three square meals on the table for their families. Finding protein was the biggest challenge, because meats were the most expensive part of a meal. Here are some of the frugal dishes eaten during the 1930s: macaroni and cheese, roast beef hash, creamed chipped beef on toast, salmon loaf, meat loaf (stretched with a filler such as oatmeal or bread crumbs), spaghetti and meatballs, oxtail soup, and Depression hot dish (bacon, onions, carrots, potatoes, and a can of cream-style corn).

However, for very poor families with many children, at times the main meal could consist of bread served with a plain soup made of flour, water, a little butter, and seasoned with salt and pepper. Others ate dandelions and wild roots when their food supplies were low.

Then, by the late thirties, life began to perk up. It looked like the economy was recovering. One indication of this was the following optimistic cookbook that came out in 1936 called *The Joy of Cooking* by Irma Rombauer (1877–1962). This Saint Louis housewife, whose husband had committed suicide at the start of the Depression in 1930, wrote and privately published a cookbook in 1931 for her family and friends. It was a collection of favorite family recipes. After Rombauer refined the original text, the Bobbs-Merrill Company, Inc., published a version of her book in 1936. It took off and became a serious contender to Fannie Farmer's cookbook.

Irma Rombauer's book was such a success because she gave down-to-earth instructions to amateur cooks like herself. She introduced a new recipe format that blended detailed directions and ingredients together. Irma guided cooks through every step. In her charming presentations, she made cooking kind of fun and less scientific. Here is an example of her easy style:

Sauté:

    1/2 lb. chopped mushrooms

In:

    2 tablespoons butter

Stir in:

    2 tablespoons flour

Rombauer's book, *The Joy of Cooking*, was a best seller by 1943. Though she died in 1962, her book was updated and revised by her daughter, Marion Rombauer Becker, until her own death in 1976. The final Rombauer-Becker edition was published in 1975. Irma's grandson, Ethan Becker, oversees updated versions written by several food writers.

By 1940 Americans were just starting to enjoy eating a variety of foods again when a portly man by the name of James Beard (1903–1985) appeared on the culinary scene with a book called *Hors D'Oeuvre & Canapés*. This former caterer's first book on hors d'oeuvre (means "outside the meal" or "appetizers"), canapés (a small appetizer such as a piece of toast with a spread on top), cocktails, and advice about entertaining has become a classic. James Beard, a knowledgeable and well-traveled man, wrote more cookbooks, opened up a cooking school, and became such an expert on American food that he turned into the United States' first food celebrity and television chef.

Deviled Eggs

Serves 6

You will need:
9 hard-boiled eggs, peeled
¾ cup mayonnaise
2 teaspoons yellow mustard
1 teaspoon dried dill weed
1 teaspoon dried celery seed
¼ teaspoon salt
¼ teaspoon pepper
¼ teaspoon paprika
paprika for garnish

Equipment:
measuring cups and spoons
kitchen knife for slicing
large serving plate
mixing bowl
electric hand mixer
small spoon

What to do:
1. Cut each egg in half lengthwise and place on large plate.
2. Carefully remove each cooked yolk from egg white halves and place in bowl.
3. Add mayonnaise, mustard, dill weed, celery seed, salt, pepper, and paprika.
4. Using electric hand mixer, mix all ingredients until fairly smooth.
5. Carefully spoon egg mixture into hollow areas of each egg white.
6. Sprinkle eggs with paprika and serve or refrigerate until eating.

Eggs Hors D'Oeuvre and James Beard:

James Beard advised in his book *Hors D'Oeuvre & Canapés* that no matter what else was served at a cocktail party, a tray of deviled eggs would always be popular and disappear the quickest. He also suggested for a fancier look, instead of a spoon, use a pastry tube to fill the halves with the yolk mixture. Besides deviled eggs, Beard provided other recipes for all kinds of stuffed eggs including anchovy eggs and pâté eggs (with duck liver paste).

War Rations and Victory Gardens

By the time the United States had declared war on Japan and Germany on December 8, 1941, many American women had already rushed into grocery stores that very morning to buy all the white sugar they could carry. The United States' entrance into the war was not unexpected, and many remembered or had heard stories of the food shortages and rationing when, in 1917, the United States entered World War I (1914–1918). These homemakers weren't taking any chances with their families' sweet tooth. Shoppers hoarded one-hundred-pound sacks of sugar in their homes while commercial users, such as bakeries, filled their warehouses. In no time, there was a major shortage of sugar because one-sixth of the United States' sugar supplies were coming from the Philippines, which was in Japanese hands in 1942. Plus, ships that transported sugar to the United States from the Caribbean were being used for shipping wartime supplies. And so rationing and price control systems (from 1942 to 1946) began with sugar, but they would eventually include many other food products because of the shortages created when supplies were sent overseas to feed the soldiers and give aid to suffering Europeans.

During World War II (1941–1945), the U.S. government not only rationed numerous food products but also nonfood items such as gasoline, oil, rubber, and metal goods. The rationing of gasoline meant that shoppers didn't have the option of driving around town to find the best prices for their groceries. But Americans thought the rationing system was fair because then everyone would have an equal chance of getting an item. So, despite the sometimes wasting and hoarding of food, plus an occasional purchase on the black market (paying an illegal amount for a rationed product to get more of it), the rationing system worked because it was the patriotic thing to do. No one wanted the ruthless leaders of Japan and Germany to win and take over the world.

When American men went off to war, women had to fill extra roles on the home front. Even middle-class homemakers were expected to grow a garden, can homegrown foods, cook healthy meals around rationed supplies, and work all day in a factory, office, restaurant, or store.

To keep this support going for the war, the Office of War Information (OWI), a federal agency started by President Franklin Delano Roosevelt, put up posters with powerful slogans in every U.S. city. These colorful prints called upon every man, woman, and child to make personal sacrifices for the national cause. The following slogan was seen on many wartime posters:

WHERE OUR MEN ARE FIGHTING
OUR FOOD IS FIGHTING
Buy wisely. Cook carefully. Store carefully. Use leftovers.

(Division of Public Inquiries, Office of War Information 1943. OWI Poster No. 35. U.S. Government Printing Office)

HOW THE RATIONING SYSTEM WORKED ♦ During World War II, the most valuable possession for Americans was their ration books. It was said at the time that if a robber broke into a home, the family diamonds would have been easier to steal than the well-hidden ration books. Here are some examples of how the books worked:

War Ration Book One, which began on May 5, 1942, contained twenty-eight stamps and was first called the Sugar Book because white sugar was the first food rationed. When the book was first issued, homemakers were asked by the ration board to give an honest statement about how much sugar they already had in their homes. This sugar wasn't taken away from them, but the stamps representing that amount were torn out of the ration book. The weekly ration for sugar started at about 8 ounces per person, but when supplies were low, the stamps could not be validated until there was enough sugar for everyone to get the specified amount. When people were permitted to obtain their portion of sugar, they would pay the price the storekeeper was asking plus have a stamp torn from their ration books.

War Ration Book Two, released in February of 1943, contained red stamps and blue stamps each worth ten points; however, point values changed monthly depending on the available supplies. The red stamps were for meats, cheese, and fats. The blue stamps were for processed foods such as canned, bottled, frozen, or dried vegetables, fruits, soups, baby food, juices, and ketchup. With the red and blue stamps, people could pick and choose what to "spend" their points on.

Here are some examples of how the points worked:

MEAT: Red stamps were needed to buy fresh, frozen, cured, or canned beef, veal, pork, and lamb, plus varieties of other meats such as sausages, hot dogs, canned fish, and poultry. Ground beef became a favorite because it was fewer points per pound than roasts or chops and could be stretched with fillers such as bread crumbs. Pork was also low in points and easier to find than some of the other meats. Fresh poultry, fish, and wild game were not rationed.

BUTTER: Of all the rationed fats, butter was the one missed the most. But many considered meat more of a necessity so some consumers went without their four ounces per week of butter rations to save their red stamps for meat. Many bought the cheaper and not rationed margarine. Before the 1960s, all margarine was white in the United States because dairy farmers and manufacturers had laws passed in several states taxing the coloring of margarine. They didn't want margarine to be yellow like butter. To get around this, margarine processors sold their product with a packet of yellow food coloring that could be kneaded into the margarine by the consumer at home. After the war, the courts removed this color barrier, and by the 1960s, tubs of yellow margarine and vegetable spreads were introduced.

Besides margarine, fats from bacon and other meats were used for cooking instead of butter. But the U.S. government tried to discourage this practice because it wanted Americans to save these cooking fats so they could be made into glycerin used for explosives in the war.

CHEESE: Cheese was rationed because much of it was being shipped to Europe. But as with their butter rations, some Americans chose to cut down on their cheese intake to save their red stamps for meat.

CANNED MILK: Fresh milk was never rationed, but canned milk was because of the metal in the can. All canned goods were rationed because either the metal was used for building airplanes, ships, weapons, and other equipment needed to fight the war or the canned goods were sent to feed the troops.

VICTORY GARDENS AND CANNING ♦ In anticipation of wartime rationing, the National Victory Garden program was launched in the United States in 1941. It wasn't anything new. The U.S. government had encouraged backyard and communal garden plots since World War I and throughout the Depression. However, a new scarcity of fresh vegetables

had occurred in California because of the relocation of Japanese Americans to internment camps during World War II. Japanese American farmers had grown two-thirds of the vegetable crop in the large state.

With this shortage of vegetables, more and more victory gardeners went out into their backyards, vacant lots, ball fields, parks, rooftops, tiny strips of land between their row houses, and even in attics to plants and harvest their crops. Pressure cookers, airtight pots for quick cooking or canning by means of superheated steam under pressure, were used for canning nonacid vegetables and meats to prevent botulism, a spore-forming bacteria that leads to food poisoning. There were so many home canners that a shortage occurred of canning equipment and neighbors had to share equipment. Plus, inexperienced home canners had to learn to use a pressure cooker, as these units were known to explode or rupture if not used properly.

All in all, the typical wartime kitchen had a bulging pantry with all the home-canned goods stacked on the shelves. Some were so proud of their canning accomplishments that they didn't want to use up their canned foods. Soon news articles were telling families : "Eat it—Don't Save It!"

Wartime Cake

Serves 6

You will need:
1 teaspoon baking soda
2 tablespoons water
1 cup firmly packed brown sugar
1⅓ cups water
½ cup vegetable shortening
1 cup raisins
½ teaspoon ground nutmeg
1 teaspoon ground cinnamon
½ teaspoon ground cloves
½ teaspoon salt
2 cups all-purpose flour
1 teaspoon baking powder
cooking spray

Equipment:
measuring cups and spoons
small bowl
large saucepan
wooden spoon
8 × 8 × 2-inch baking pan
spatula
2 pot holders
wire rack
cake cutter

What to do:
1. Preheat oven to 325°F.

2. In small bowl, dissolve baking soda in 2 tablespoons of water. Put aside.

3. In large saucepan, mix brown sugar, 1⅓ cups water, shortening, raisins, nutmeg, cinnamon, and cloves with wooden spoon.

4. Bring saucepan to boil over medium-high heat. Boil for 3 minutes. Take off heat and let cool.

5. Mix salt and baking soda solution into a saucepan.
6. Blend in flour and baking powder.
7. Grease baking pan with cooking spray.
8. Pour cake batter into baking pan, scraping saucepan with spatula.

9. Bake cake for 30 to 40 minutes, or until middle is springy to touch.
10. Remove from oven with pot holders and cool on wire rack.
11. Cut into squares and serve.

Americans Never Gave Up Their Sweet Tooth

Americans first ate cakes like this during World War I when shortages were also common. Then, in 1942, recipes for wartime cakes appeared again and were often presented as "eggless, milkless, and butterless" and delicious "un-iced."

As Americans had a hard time giving up their sweet tooth, booklets, magazines and newspaper articles advised homemakers to substitute more available and cheaper sweeteners such as brown sugar, molasses, honey, maple syrup, corn syrup, fruit juice, or marshmallows in their desserts. Though for special occasions, such as a wedding, friends and family would put all their rationed white sugar together for the wedding cake.

TV Dinners and Fast-Food Beginnings

After all the rationing, cooking, and canning of the 1940s, the 1950s arrived with a different attitude. It said: "Make it fast and make it easy." Cooking from scratch had lost its appeal. This change in cooking came on after World War II ended in 1945 and women were fired from their high-paying jobs so that the returning soldiers could replace them.

As a result of this change in job status, poorer women went back to low-paying jobs to support their families and middle-class women had little choice but to return to their homes full-time. However, they were happy to discover that keeping a house in the 1950s was becoming less labor intensive. Convenience foods allowed them to give up canning because they could purchase commercially canned and frozen goods at one of the new supermarkets popping up in every neighborhood. Casseroles made totally of canned foods allowed for easy meal preparation. Desserts became a breeze with the new cake mixes on the market, introduced in 1949 by General Mills and Pillsbury. Steaks were now affordable, and the new custom of barbecuing them on the weekends was taken over by their husbands. Plus with more kitchen appliances available to all American women, including those in rural areas, the time spent in the kitchen cooking and cleaning up afterward dropped below twenty hours a week.

Despite all these changes, the introduction of the following two milestones made the biggest impact on the United States' busier and more mobile dining culture:

TV DINNERS: In 1953 someone working for the Swanson Company (a wholesale grocery firm started in 1899) had made a big mistake. He had overestimated how many Thanksgiving turkeys the American public would buy. As a result, 260 tons of frozen turkeys sat inside ten refrigerated railroad cars. What in the world was the company going to do with them?

Fortunately, Swanson had in their employ a clever salesman by the name of Gerry Thomas. Thinking of airline food with its preprepared meal trays, Thomas ordered five-thousand aluminum trays to make a complete turkey dinner in one package. After designing the trays with three compartments, Thomas got help with the menu and required cooking technique from Swanson's food technologist, Betty Cronin. She devised a way to blanch, boil briefly, each ingredient at a different rate before freezing it so that when the consumer cooked the food, the entire meal was ready at the same time.

Swanson ordered these dinners to be put together by an assembly line of women with spatulas and ice-cream scoops. They placed turkey slices and corn-bread stuffing with gravy in the largest compartment, peas topped with butter in the second one, and whipped sweet potatoes enhanced with orange juice and butter in the third. This square meal sold for ninety-eight cents. The new black-and-white TVs appearing all over the United States in the 1950s inspired Swanson to call these frozen meals TV dinners because of their square shape.

Swanson made another mistake by doubting that the first order of TV dinners would sell, but this time it was a happy mistake. Swanson sold ten million turkey dinners in its first year of full production in 1954!

After a year on the market, the sweet potatoes were replaced with white mashed potatoes because the original potatoes were watery. The stuffing was also replaced with white-bread dressing. By 1960 a fourth compartment was added to contain cranberry sauce to make it a complete all-American meal. Though turkey remained the most popular of these frozen dinners, fried chicken, and Salisbury steak dinners were also made available. Then in 1984, the aluminum trays for these meals in a box were replaced with a paper one suitable for microwaves.

Though the package was made to look like a TV, Swanson didn't intend for people to eat their dinners in front of the set, but that's what most Americans did.

FAST-FOOD BEGINNINGS: Believe it or not, Americans were not that crazy about eating hamburgers in the early 1900s. Ground beef was considered a low-grade form of meat and a dangerous one at that, because of the unsanitary conditions at some big city meatpacking plants. Some people came down with bacterial infections, such as E. coli, that caused vomiting, diarrhea, and sometimes death. Pork was considered a safer bet and was the number one selling meat. However, some enterprising men changed our minds about the lowly hamburger.

WHITE CASTLE HAMBURGER STANDS ♦ In 1921 Edgar Waldo "Billy" Ingram, an insurance and real-estate agent, partnered with a cook named Walter Anderson to open the first White Castle Hamburger Stand in Wichita, Kansas. Though this hamburger chain began way before the 1950s, it has to be mentioned because it was the first and it's still going strong. Inside a 10- by 15-foot cement block building with five counter stools, Anderson cooked five-cent burgers. The *White* and *Castle* were put in the name to let the public know the food was clean and safe. To promote this claim, the kitchen was placed within view of the customers so they could see that the government-inspected beef patties were fresh.

In 1924 Ingram and Anderson incorporated, turning their full business name into White Castle System of Eating Houses. By 1925, still going for the "white and clean" image, newer establishments were built to look like toy castles covered with white enamel paint inside and out.

In 1933 Ingram bought out Anderson's interest in the up-and-coming hamburger stand. By 1954 a billion White Castle burgers had been sold to the American public, since its opening in 1921. Though still mainly a midwestern chain, White Castle owns and distributes frozen and microwaveable burgers all over the United States and is run by Ingram's grandson, E. W. Ingram III.

BIRTH OF MCDONALD'S ♦ A more dramatic turn of events occurred to the fast-food business in 1954 when a milk-shake machine salesman, by the name of Ray Kroc (1902–1984), walked into a San Bernardino, California, drive-in restaurant (the original McDonald's restaurant that opened in 1948) owned by the McDonald brothers, Richard and Maurice. Kroc wanted to meet the men who had ordered ten milk-shake machines for their hamburger stand. He saw firsthand their unique "Speedee Service System" that provided speed, lower prices (fifteen-cent hamburgers and ten-cent fries), and volume. In fact, Kroc liked their system so much that he talked the brothers into selling him the franchise rights. As you know, the rest is history. Ray Kroc opened his first golden arches franchise on April 15, 1955, in Des Plaines, Illinois. By 1961 Ray Kroc bought the McDonalds out for $2.7 million. The sale did not include the original San Bernardino, California, McDonald's drive-in. Eventually, Kroc would turn his hamburger stands into a worldwide company that would include thirty thousand restaurants and serve fifty million people a day. Though most Americans can still recite this commercial ditty: "Two all-beef patties, special sauce, lettuce, cheese, pickles, onions on a sesame seed bun!" other countries have slightly different menus at their local McDonald's. In India, diners enjoy "two all-lamb patties, special sauce . . ." In Japan the chicken sandwich is topped with soy sauce and ginger, and in New Zealand, a fried egg and a slice of beet tops the burger.

How White Castle and McDonald's Cook Their Burgers

A White Castle burger is a 3-inch square patty. By 1942 White Castle had added five holes to the patty to help the meat cook more evenly. As the burger is steamed on a griddle, shredded onions are placed on top of the patty. When done, it is enclosed with a pickle in a moist bun. Customers started calling these steam-grilled burgers "slyders" and the fries that accompanied them "spikes."

Under the original speedy McDonald's system, burgers were cooked on a "clamshell fryer" that heated both sides of the patty at the same time in less than four minutes. To meet the high customer demand, the burgers were cooked in batches, dressed with pickles, lettuce, tomato, onions, condiments, put in a bun, wrapped, and then placed under a heat lamp to wait for the next order. This system was fast and worked fine for decades, but by the 1980s, the system developed problems. There was waste, plus customers who didn't want a pickle or a tomato on their burgers had to wait forever for a "special order." The food also suffered. It was either cold, or the heat lamps wilted the lettuce and tomatoes.

The problem was solved in 1998 when a new " assemble to order" system was put into play. Cooked patties were placed in a new holding cabinet until ready to be assembled with a bun toasted in a new flash toaster in just eleven seconds. The total time under the new system took thirty-five seconds to make the entire hamburger sandwich. So requests such as "hold the pickles" no longer means waiting a long time, and everyone likes the burgers even better.

Double Cheeseburgers

Makes 2 double cheeseburgers

You will need:
1 pound lean ground beef
salt and pepper
2 white onion slices
2 hamburger buns
4 slices of American cheese
2 tomato slices

4 slices of dill pickle
2 cups of shredded
   iceberg lettuce
mustard
mayonnaise
ketchup

Equipment:
measuring cup
large griddle
spatula
kitchen knife
2 small plates

What to do:
1. Place large griddle on stove and heat to medium high.

2. Divide meat into quarters.

3. Sprinkle salt and pepper on meat before shaping each quarter into a ball. Will have 4 meatballs.

4. Place the meatballs on griddle, and flatten each meatball with the spatula until they form hamburger patties. Cook for several minutes, and then flip over patties and continue cooking.

5. Place 2 onion slices on griddle and brown.

6. Open up buns and place each side down on griddle to lightly toast.

7. When patties are cooked all the way through and no pink remains in the middle, add a slice of cheese on top of each patty.

8. Use spatula to put 2 patties together, 1 on top of the other. Do the same with the other 2 patties.

9. Place each double cheeseburger on a bottom bun.

10. Lay a browned onion slice on the top of each.

11. Add 1 tomato slice, 2 pickle slices, and 1 cup of lettuce on each.

12. Put on the top buns, enclosing each double cheeseburger.

Serve immediately with condiments (mayonnaise, mustard, ketchup).

Years of Great
Culinary Advances:

1960–1989

Mastering French Cooking and Other International Cuisines

By 1960 popular cookbooks like *The I Hate to Cook Book* (1960) by Peg Bracken were still encouraging homemakers to use prepackaged products such as noodles and canned soups to make meals quick and easy. But that was soon to change when an American woman who had studied French cooking in France appeared on the culinary scene. When Julia Child (1912–2004) returned to the United States in the 1960s, she brought great French cuisine into the kitchen and rescued Americans from their boring array of bland casseroles.

Just as Julia Child's book *Mastering the Art of French Cooking* (co-authored with Louisette Bertholle and Simone Beck) came out in 1961, the growing middle class in the United States was traveling for the first time in jets to far-off places such as Paris and southern France. In these exciting locales, Americans began to experience the great French cuisine. So when they came home, they were ready to learn how to cook French food. Adding to this high interest in everything French was the hiring of a

French chef in 1960 by First Lady Jacqueline Lee Bouvier Kennedy to do the cooking in the White House.

Julia and her French coauthors made French cooking sound simple and approachable in their book. Julia wrote comforting words of encouragement: "You don't have to cook fancy or complicated masterpieces—just good food from fresh ingredients." The book also promised that "anyone can cook in the French manner anywhere, with the right instruction." The authors also advised that to make delicious meals one cannot eliminate steps or skimp on time or ingredients like cream and butter.

Mastering the Art of French Cooking is still popular because of its unique approach in the following ways: It leads experienced and beginner cooks with clear, detailed steps in each recipe from how to buy and handle raw ingredients to making the final creation. It adapts classical techniques to modern American kitchen appliances. The book also shows Americans how to buy products, from any supermarket, that will reproduce the exact taste and texture of the French ingredient.

Following the fame from this book, Julia Child, went on to host a cooking show, *The French Chef*, on Boston's educational television station in 1963. This fifty-year-old, six-foot-two, freckle-faced woman with a high-pitched voice that warbled, won over an American audience because of her cheery personality, clear instructions, passion for good food, and funny mishaps. She once spilled some of a potato dish onto a stove top during her show. She simply put it back in the pan, telling the audience it was okay to serve because no one would know. She also always ended each show with a happy, "Bon appétit!" (good appetite).

In addition to French cooking, the average American in the 1960s, who had enough money to travel to faraway countries, began to be interested in other ethnic foods. This interest became even more pronounced when the Immigration Act of 1965 allowed a new wave of immigrants with their own unique eating customs to enter the United States. The following are some of these newer immigrants and their special foods:

KOREANS: Kimchi (pickled vegetables like fermented cabbage and cucumbers) is served with almost every Korean meal.

FILIPINOS: Lumpia is the Filipino version of the Chinese egg roll.

VIETNAMESE: Favorite dishes served with noodles or rice are beef soup and lemongrass chicken.

CAMBODIANS: Specialties include raw fish salad and sweet pork and egg (the blending of meat with sugar or sweet things is a common practice in the Cambodian culture).

THAI: Some favorite dishes are pad Thai (stir-fry rice noodles) and Tom Yum Kung (very spicy hot soup).

INDIANS: Immigrants from India favor basmati rice with its rich and nutty flavor. The Indians are also known for their spice blends of ginger, coriander seeds, cinnamon, black peppercorns, turmeric, red pepper flakes, and garlic.

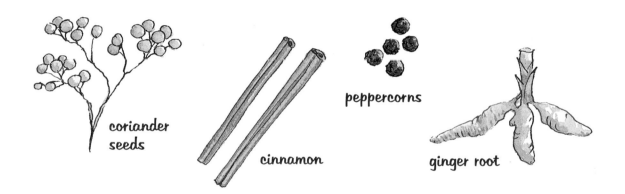

coriander seeds

cinnamon

peppercorns

ginger root

Quiche

Makes 2 pies (4 to 6 servings each)

You will need:

For piecrusts:
1½ cups all-purpose flour
½ teaspoon salt
1 cup butter (2 sticks)
⅓ cup cold water
flour for dusting

For filling:
1 tablespoon butter
½ cup finely chopped white onion
3 eggs slightly beaten
2 cups cream
1 teaspoon salt
½ pound swiss cheese, cut into small pieces
¼ pound (4 slices) boiled ham cut into small pieces
1 cup chopped broccoli crown (no stem)
cayenne
nutmeg

Equipment:
large mixing bowl
measuring cups and spoons
wooden spoon
pastry cutter
kitchen fork
board to roll dough
rolling pin
2 (9-inch) glass pie plates
skillet
dish towel
2 pot holders
2 wire racks

What to do:

1. Mix flour and salt in large bowl. Add butter and cut with pastry cutter until mixture looks like coarse cornmeal.

2. Pour water in and mix with fork until dough sticks together in a ball.

3. Divide ball in half and roll each ball out with rolling pin, one at a time, on floured board until each one is 1 inch or so wider than pie plate.

4. Fold both over and lay one in each pie plate. Unfold and press dough lightly on bottom and sides of plates. Flute (pleat) edges with fingers.

5. With fork, lightly prick bottom and sides of dough in each pie plate. Set dough-lined pie plates aside.

6. Preheat oven to 450°F.

7. Stirring with wooden spoon, sauté butter and onions in skillet for 5 minutes.

8. Rinse out mixing bowl and dry before putting in eggs, cream, salt, cheese, ham, and broccoli.

9. Add onions.

10. Sprinkle a dash of cayenne and nutmeg into mixture before blending well with wooden spoon.

11. Carefully pour mixture into each unbaked piecrust, making sure cheese, ham, and broccoli are evenly distributed in each pie. Pour mixture not more than three-fourths full in each pie shell, as quiche will puff up during baking.

12. Bake pies for 10 minutes at 450°F, then reduce temperature to 325°F and cook until firm, about 25 minutes, or until knife inserted in middle of pie comes out clean.

13. Remove from oven with pot holders and place on wire racks.

14. Serve warm but not piping hot. However, a cold quiche makes a good snack and can be taken on picnics. Cut into wedges when serving.

Note: Cooked bacon can be substituted for the ham in this recipe. Plus the broccoli can be left out. Or invent your own combinations.

The Popularity of Quiche

Quiche didn't really become the rage in the United States until the late 1960s. By the 1980s, quiche had grown so popular that chefs began to compete with one another to invent new recipes with anchovies or yams. But those creations couldn't compare to the classic quiche Lorraine (made with eggs, cream, and bacon) or recipes such as the vegetable, ham, and cheese quiche combination.

Popular Food Movements:
Vegetarianism & Mexican American Cookery

While Julia Child was whipping up French dishes such as coq au vin (chicken with mushrooms, onions, bacon, and red wine) and crêpes suzette (thin pancakes rolled in an orange butter, which are sprinkled with liquor and set on fire before serving), two other food movements were on the rise.

The first of these movements was created in the late 1960s by a growing social unrest in the United States due to the Vietnam War (1957–1975). As a result of these tensions, hippies, young people who rejected violence and shunned the establishment, appeared on the scene, protesting the war and introducing a different way of life. Many of these "flower children" lived in communes, settlements where people shared property and goods, and ate only unprocessed foods. They created a "back-to-scratch" movement by making their own bread, peanut butter, hummus (a paste of pureed chickpeas), and granola.

Many Americans called these war protesters granola heads because of their vegetarian diets (they thought it cruel to kill animals for food). But soon mainstream Americans became curious enough to venture out and try some "hippie foods." A lot of them found the herbal teas, bean sprouts, and vegetarian fare to their liking. As a result, restaurants started sprouting up, offering delicious vegetarian dishes such as meatless chili, veggie burgers, tofu stir-fry, zucchini bread, carrot cake, whole grain breads, and many homemade pasta and brown rice dishes.

With vegetarianism becoming popular in the United States, people began to realize that not all vegetarians are alike. The following is a list of the different types:

VEGAN: Consumes no animal flesh (meat, fish, poultry, or fish) and avoids all foods of animal origin. Some will not eat honey or wear animal products, such as leather shoes.

OVO-LACTO VEGETARIAN: Consumes no animal flesh but does eat eggs and milk products (the most popular form of vegetarianism)

LACTO VEGETARIAN: Consumes no animal flesh and eggs but does eat milk products

FRUITARIANS: Consumes only fruits, nuts, and seeds. They will not eat root vegetables such as potatoes or carrots because the plant is killed. But they will eat fruit like apples or oranges because they can be picked without killing the plant.

The second food trend to take off in the 1960s was Mexican American cuisine with its spicy dishes. Though Mexican Americans have been in America for centuries, their delicious foods were not nationally known until a man named Glen W. Bell Jr. came along with four hundred dollars in his pocket and an idea about serving tacos as a fast food. He founded Taco Bell in 1962, opening the first one in Downey, California.

As you know, Bell's Mexican fast-food concept became a chain of successful eateries, making him a millionaire. In 1978 he sold his company to PepsiCo for $125 million.

Though Taco Bell may not offer authentic regional Mexican cooking, it has done more than any other Mexican eating establishment in exposing new flavors and textures to an American public that would not have otherwise tried them.

Frito-Lay also promoted Mexican American food by introducing in 1966, Doritos, a corn chip that went so well with a growing passion in the United States for salsas (spicy sauce of tomatoes, onions, and chili peppers).

These different food movements sometimes warred against each other in the 1960s, but before the twentieth century ended and the twenty-first began, the United States' maturing and diversified culinary tastes produced more and more imaginative cooks.

Vegetarian Burritos

Makes 4 burritos

You will need
1 (3½-ounce) boil-in-a-bag brown rice
1 quart water
1 cup chunky salsa
1 (15-ounce) can black beans, rinsed and drained
4 (10-inch) flour tortillas made with vegetable oil
½ cup canned vegetarian refried beans
1 cup shredded Monterey Jack cheese
   with jalapeño peppers
2 peeled avocados, each cut into 6 slices
¼ cup sour cream
8 cilantro sprigs
1 lime cut into 4 wedges

Equipment:
2-quart microwave-safe bowl
tongs
kitchen knife
small mixing bowl
measuring cups and spoons
skillet
wooden spoon
paper towels
4 plates
small spoon

What to do:
1. Submerge 1 bag of rice in bowl with water. Microwave for 10 minutes.

2. Carefully remove bag with tongs and drain. Cut open and empty bag of rice into small bowl. Set aside.

3. Combine salsa and black beans in skillet with wooden spoon. Cook over medium heat for 5 minutes, or until heated throughout.

4. Stack tortillas before wrapping in damp paper towels. Microwave for 25 seconds or until warm.

5. Lay each tortilla on a plate. Using a small spoon, spread 2 tablespoons of refried beans over each tortilla.

6. Top each with ½ cup rice, ½ cup bean and salsa mixture, ¼ cup cheese, 3 avocado slices, 1 tablespoon sour cream, and 2 cilantro sprigs.

7. Roll up each filled tortilla. Cut in half and serve with lime wedges.

Note: These are large burritos, and each one may serve two if so desired.
   Also, if you are serving a vegan, leave out the cheese and sour cream.

Organic Produce and More Food Trends

Whenever Alice Waters, chef, restaurateur, and cookbook author, finds a snail in her fresh vegetables, she is delighted. Why? Well, because it means the produce has been organically grown (free of synthetic pesticides and fertilizers). Her philosophy of using organically grown food eaten only in season became such a hit nationally in the 1970s that a new movement called California cuisine was born.

Alice Waters's love of good food began when she was a young American woman living in France. In 1971 Waters was so inspired by what she had eaten in France that she used French recipes with California ingredients when she opened her own restaurant, Chez Panisse, in Berkeley, California. All the dishes at this still famous eating establishment are made of "real food grown by people who are taking care of the land." Waters wants her patrons to feel like they are enjoying a dinner party at home with friends and family.

She makes sure fresh fruit and vegetables are picked daily, various meats and dairy products are obtained from local ranches and dairies, and that fish comes straight out of the sea. What Alice can't grow herself, she buys at farmers' markets, where locally grown produce can be purchased and used right away. (Europeans have been doing this for centuries.) In fact, Alice made farmers' markets so popular that more and more growers around the United States are selling their crops at outdoor markets set up in cities and towns on the weekends or during certain weekdays. This practice has served a real community service in some low-income urban areas where often only one store serves a large community and fresh produce is only available through these visiting farmers' markets.

In addition to Alice Waters, other celebrity chefs and culinary trends were making their own statements at the start of the 1980s. Wolfgang Puck was one of these chefs who won popularity and fame with the opening of his restaurant Spago on Sunset Boulevard in Los Angeles. In his open kitchen, he introduced oven-fired gourmet pizzas, Asian fusion cooking (the blending of Eastern and Western influences and cooking techniques), and many other delicious dishes using fresh ingredients.

Even with all this coming and going of food trends, Americans still held onto their passion for anything Italian. But despite this love for fresh pasta dishes, garlic, olive oil, and pizza pies, another ethnic cuisine called Tex-Mex was gaining ground. The Tex-Mex movement was born from the culinary joining of Spain, Mexico, and the American Southwest. It is a combination of northern Mexican peasant food and Texas farm and cowboy fare. A great example of this cuisine is the fajita, a dish made of marinated grilled steak, onions, and peppers served with warm tortillas.

Peach Cobbler

Serves 6 to 8

You will need:

Fruit filling:
12 medium to large organic freestone peaches, peeled and sliced
2 tablespoons unbleached all-purpose flour
1 teaspoon cinnamon
sugar for sprinkling
½ cup (1 stick) unsalted butter

Soft crust:
1½ cups unbleached all-purpose flour
2 teaspoons baking powder
1½ cups sugar
1½ cups milk

Equipment:
9 × 13 baking pan
measuring cups and spoons
wooden spoon
mixing bowl
wire whisk
spatula
pot holders
cooling rack

What to do:

1. Preheat oven to 350°F.

2. Place peach slices in baking pan. Add flour, cinnamon, and a sprinkling of sugar to peaches, mixing gently with spoon.

3. Break stick of butter into small chunks with fingers and dot top of peaches. Set aside.

4. Mix together flour, baking powder, sugar, and milk in bowl with wire whisk until smooth like pancake batter.

5. Pour batter over peaches, scraping bowl with spatula.

6. Bake in oven for 1 hour, or until crust is a golden brown and fruit is cooked.

7. Remove carefully with pot holders and place on cooling rack.

Serve warm with vanilla ice cream, preferably homemade.

Dining, Cooking, and Eating
into the Twenty-First Century:

1990–21st Century

Hold the Fat, Hold the Cholesterol, Hold the Carbs

As the 1990s were closing in on the twenty-first century, the United States found itself with a major health issue: obesity. Busy Americans (many women were working and not cooking as much) were dining on foods such as deep-fried chicken, thick slices of pizza, double cheeseburgers, and big slabs of steak. Restaurant and take-out orders were supersized to meet the demands of a public becoming used to fatty, high-calorie meals. In addition, junk food (snack foods with no nutritional value) such as sodas, chips, doughnuts, candy, and cookies (even deep-fried Oreo cookies) were purchased and enjoyed at an alarming rate. Wise and humorous quotes such as the following brought this weighty issue home to many Americans:

Never eat more than you can lift.
—Miss Piggy (a muppet)

My doctor told me to stop having intimate dinners for four.
Unless there are three other people.
—Orson Welles (1915–1985, actor, writer, filmmaker)

Joking aside, most Americans came to realize that being fat meant more than not fitting into their jeans. According to the Centers for Disease Control and Prevention, obesity is a serious condition that can lead to diabetes and heart disease when a person is overweight by more than twenty pounds.

To add to the woes of Americans with expanding waistlines, they were told of the health dangers of trans-fatty acids (an artery-clogging fat formed when hydrogen is added to liquid vegetable oils to make them solid.) Not only were trans-fatty acids found in fast foods like french fries and other fried offerings, but they were also in processed foods such as doughnuts, cookies, pastries, cereals, and waffles. The Food and Drug Administration (FDA) ruled in favor of making food manufacturers list trans fat on their labels, starting in 2006.

To fight this fat battle, many Americans raced to gyms to get on treadmills and stationary bicycles to burn it off. They also ate new food products with reduced fat, low fat, fat free, carb free, no cholesterol (animal fat), and artificial sweeteners. However, because many Americans overate these diet foods, they found that not only were the pounds not coming off but they were packing on more.

Many overweight Americans thought the answer to their problems was to go on a fad diet and get the weight off fast. However, some dieters simply couldn't stick with the restrictive plans or they'd lose the weight and then gain it back quickly. The following are a list of three of these popular diets:

ATKINS DIET: A low-carbohydrate weight-loss plan that only allows 20 grams of carbs (example: 1 cup of cooked spinach = 20 grams of carbs) per day during the first two weeks. The dieter eats a high concentration of meat, eggs, cheese, and bacon. Then after the two weeks, more carbs are allowed until 40 to 90 grams per day are reached for maintenance control.

THE ZONE: A low-calorie diet with strict portion control. It depends on a scientific calculation of how many grams of protein and carbohydrates to eat per day to lose weight while maintaining energy.

SOUTH BEACH DIET: A low carbohydrate diet that clears the dieter of "bad" carbohydrates (potatoes, white bread, etc.) and saturated fats that lead to weight gain. It recommends "good" carbs (whole grains and vegetables) that take longer to break down in the body and promote weight loss.

When none of the above methods worked for the high-risk morbidly obese (overweight by one hundred-plus pounds), some elected to undergo an operation called the Roux-en-Y gastric bypass. This operation makes the stomach smaller by creating a small pouch at the top of the stomach with surgical staples or a plastic band. The smaller stomach is connected to the middle portion of the small intestine, bypassing the rest of the stomach and the upper portion of the small intestine. This results in fewer calories being absorbed and leads to weight loss.

Despite all these desperate measures to lose weight in the 1990s and in the present, there are moderate Americans who choose to ignore fad diets, excessive exercise routines, and surgeries. Instead, they dine on healthier cuisines with less fat, such as Pacific Rim fare that offers sushi and sashimi (rice and raw fish) as one of its specialties. They also cook with "super foods" (known for their disease-fighting properties and extra nutrition), such as nuts, soy products, yogurt, and whole grain cereals and breads.

These healthy Americans are also guided by a "Slow Food Movement" (started in Italy in 1986) that holds to similar beliefs as those of Alice Waters and many Europeans in preserving local cuisines and ingredients and discouraging the eating of processed foods, including mass-produced, fast-food burgers and fries.

The U.S. Department of Agriculture has also tried to offer, as it has done in the past, guides for better eating. After it reduced the Basic Seven food group (created during World War II) to the Basic Four in 1956 and created a food pyramid in 1992 to reduce the fat, especially saturated fat, in Americans' diets, the government decided to do away with the one-size-fits-all pyramid in 2005. It came up with a dozen different pyramids geared toward individual nutritional needs and lifestyles. Grains and vegetables are still the largest recommended portions in all the guides. Exercise is also emphasized with the new system.

Pumpkin Muffins

9 muffins

You will need:
2 cups unbleached all-purpose flour
2 teaspoons baking soda
2½ teaspoons cinnamon
1 teaspoon baking powder
½ teaspoon salt
4 eggs
2 cups sugar
1 cup canola oil
2 cups canned pure pumpkin
cooking oil spray

Equipment:
measuring cups and spoons
2 mixing bowls
wooden spoon
spatula
2 (6-cup) muffin tins
pot holders
cooling racks
small knife

What to do:
1. Preheat oven to 350° degrees.

2. In mixing bowl, mix flour, soda, cinnamon, baking powder, and salt with wooden spoon. Set aside.

3. In the other bowl, add eggs, sugar, and oil, beating with wooden spoon until well mixed. Add to flour mixture, stirring well.

4. Blend in pumpkin.

5. Spray muffin tins with cooking oil.

6. Fill each cup with muffin batter until two-thirds full. In the second muffin tin, you will run out of batter to fill every cup. Pour a little bit of water in the empty cups to protect tin from burning and to keep the rest of the muffins moist.

7. Bake in oven for about 30 minutes, or until a knife inserted in the middle of a muffin comes out clean.

8. Remove muffin tins from oven using pot holders and cool on racks for 5 minutes. Run knife around each muffin to loosen before carefully removing muffins from tins.

Serve warm with or without butter.

The Goodness of Pumpkin

A pumpkin is a vegetable low in calories and rich in fiber, potassium, riboflavin, and vitamins C and E. Pumpkins are also full of carotenoids (yellow to red pigments found in plants and animals), such as alpha carotene, beta-carotene, and lutein. Carotenoids are thought to protect the body against heart disease and cancer and may prevent age-related vision loss.

The Future of American Cooking and Eating

What will Americans be eating in the future? Do you think fast foods will fade away? What types of foods will be the rage according to the restaurant industry? What ethnic food will become the most popular? Will we learn to cook and eat foods from cultures we know little about? What new technologies will affect how Americans eat in their homes and in restaurants? And what of the health issue that continues to haunt American society—combating obesity?

Here are a few predictions about what could happen in the United States' culinary future:

Most food experts generally agree that fast food isn't about to disappear anytime soon. Many fast-food franchises are keeping up with the times by offering salads, chicken sandwiches, yogurts, and fresh fruit for those customers who want something healthier than the traditional burger and fries. They are also working on reducing their levels of trans-fatty acids in their cooking. However, most fast-food profits come from the "heavy users" defined as young men between the ages of eighteen and thirty-four who eat burgers, fries, and other fast-food offerings four or five times a week. But who knows, maybe some of these men might be swayed toward a veggie burger (meatless). Some see the soy-based vegan burger making a big splash in the years to come as a fast food. With this in mind, a tiny chain called Mr. Goodburgers has high hopes of making it big in California with its vegan burger joints.

Besides the hamburger, the restaurant industry forecasts that handheld foods such as sandwiches, doughnuts, pizza, and bagels are a growing industry that will become even more popular with the American people.

As to what ethnic food will become the overwhelming favorite by the middle of the twenty-first century, many are saying it will be Mexican American fare all the way from authentic regional cooking to Taco Bell. This prediction is based on the ever-increasing population of Latinos (Spanish-speaking people) in the United States who are mostly from Mexico. At the present time, Mexican, Italian, and Chinese foods are the top three restaurant cuisines in the United States.

Besides the larger ethnic groups in the United States, hopefully, we will learn more about other foreign cultures and their foods in the future, such as those of Egypt and southern Africa.

In addition to the foods of the future, what of the technology needed to deliver this diverse fare? Would it someday be possible to order foods from anywhere in the world on the Internet and have them delivered within minutes piping hot to your door? Or what about ordering off a computer at a restaurant instead of with a waiter or waitress?

But the overwhelming question for the future is how to deal with the obesity problem in the United States, despite everyone's good intentions. With the present national concern about weight, many food companies, besides the fast-food industry, are offering healthier products. Companies such as Frito-Lay switched from hydrogenated oils containing trans-fatty acids to corn oil in making Doritos and other chips. Despite these attempts to prevent people from becoming fat, fad diets are still around. Will these

quick and temporary fixes ever go away? Will science come up with a pill to keep people thin or somehow alter their fat genes? Some of these scientific innovations for losing fat may come to pass. But in the meantime, after studying a host of diets in 1999, the USDA had come to the following conclusion: "The secret of permanent weight loss is to eat less and exercise more."

Though we don't know with any certainty what will happen in the future, we do know that Americans have traveled quite a culinary road in the last century. In the twenty-first century, with recipes being downloaded on the Internet, prepared by TV chefs such as Emeril Lagasse on the Food Network, and written about in magazines and books, your family has a lot of choices to make. But no matter what you eat, keep the following quote in mind:

Preach not to others what they should eat,

but eat as becomes you, and be silent.

—Epictetus

(55–135, Greek teacher and philosopher)

Fool Medames

(Egyptian bean dish)

Serves 4

You will need:

1 cup dried small fava beans
    (found at Middle Eastern import stores)
1 tablespoon dried red lentils
    (found at Middle Eastern import stores)
1 quart water
½ cup olive oil
1 tablespoon fresh lemon juice
1 teaspoon salt
1 tablespoon finely chopped parsley
8 pitted Kalamata olives or other
    Mediterranean-type olives

Equipment:

measuring cups and spoons
colander
heavy 3- to 4-quart
    saucepan with lid
wooden spoon
fork
2 mixing bowls
wire whisk
small plates

What to do:

1. Wash beans and lentils in colander under cold running water. Drain thoroughly.
2. Pour water into saucepan and bring to a boil over high heat. Add beans and lentils.
3. Reduce heat and partially cover pot. Simmer for 3 to 4 hours.
4. Stir with wooden spoon occasionally, and check to make sure beans remain moist.
5. You may need to add a few tablespoons of hot water to the pot if beans are dry.
6. When beans can be gently poked with fork and almost all the water is gone, they are done.
7. Carefully pour beans and lentils into mixing bowl. Let cool to room temperature.
8. In the other mixing bowl, whisk oil, lemon juice, and salt together.
9. Pour over beans and lentils, mashing gently with fork. Stir dressing well into bean mixture.
10. Serve on individual small plates after sprinkling with parsley and garnishing with olives.

Note: This can also be eaten with hard-boiled eggs.

Fool: An Egyptian Staple

Fool medames (also spelled *ful medames*) is a nourishing dish sold on the streets of Egypt or in fool shops. It is a traditional breakfast food. Egyptians call this dish "the poor man's meat" even though fool is also served at the best restaurants in Egypt.

Appendix

Additional directions for using recipes in the classroom with your teacher and thirty-two classmates:

Chapter 1
Deviled eggs: need another mixing bowl, electric hand mixer, spoon, and knife for slicing. Increase ingredients: double recipe and serve each classmate half an egg.

Chapter 2
Wartime cake: need portable toaster oven, one more bowl, saucepan, spoon, baking pan, spatula, extra pot holders, small paper plates, and plastic forks. Increase ingredients: make two recipes for two cakes and cut into small squares.

Chapter 3
Double cheeseburgers: need one large electric griddle, paper plates, plastic forks and knives. Increase ingredients: 16 pounds lean ground beef, 8 onions sliced, 64 slices American cheese, 8 heads of iceberg lettuce shredded, 8 tomatoes sliced, 64 slices dill pickles, and 32 hamburger buns.

Chapter 4
Quiche: need portable toaster oven, two more 9-inch glass pie plates, electric frying pan, pastry cutter, extra fork, rolling pin, board, dish towels, pot holders, and wire racks. Increase ingredients: make two recipes for four pies, cutting each pie into eight slices.

Chapter 5
Vegetarian burritos: need another 2-quart microwave-safe bowl, tongs, extra wooden and small spoons, mixing bowl, electric frying pan, paper plates, and plastic forks and knives. Increase ingredients: double recipe, making eight burritos. Cut each burrito into four pieces.

Chapter 6
Peach cobbler: need portable toaster oven, another 9 × 13 baking pan, extra wooden spoon, mixing bowl, wire whisk, spatula, pot holders, cooking racks, small plastic bowls, and plastic forks and spoons. Increase ingredients: make two recipes for two cobblers. Will make thirty-two small servings.

Chapter 7
Pumpkin muffins: need portable toaster oven, two more 6-cup muffin tins, two more mixing bowls, extra wooden spoon, spatula, cooling racks, and pot holders. Increase ingredients: make two recipes for eighteen muffins. Cut each muffin in half.

Chapter 8
Fool Medames: need two portable electric burners, another heavy 3- to 4-quart saucepan with lid, extra wooden spoon, fork, mixing bowls, wire whisk, paper bowls, and plastic spoons. Increase ingredients: double recipe and serve small portions.

Source Notes

In researching the evolution of the United States' diverse culinary history, I found fascinating information from cookbooks, magazine articles, newspaper clippings, and the Internet. When writing chapters 1, 2, 3, and 4, two volumes stood out as the most valuable. The first of these texts, *American Century Cookbook: The Most Popular Recipes of the 20th Century* by Jean Anderson, I referred to often when confirming information gathered from other texts. This book gave me such a great overview and timeline of all the culinary innovations that took place during the early to mid 1900s. The second volume, *The Food Chronology* by James Trager, is a detailed reference book listing not only dates from prehistoric times to 1995 in regard to the cultural development of food but it also provides anecdotes about people, politics, inventions, and historical events that shaped how people all over the world eat today.

Other texts, such as *Stories and Recipes of the Great Depression of the 1930s*, vol. 3, by Rita Van Amber, helped me with information about the Great Depression in chapter 1. In chapter 2, *Grandma's Wartime Kitchen* by Joanne Lamb Hayes was a great source of information about war rationing. In chapter 3, an article in the *Modesto Bee* newspaper by Don Babwin from the Associated Press, "A Truly Golden Anniversary for These Arches" gave a wonderful fifty-year history of McDonald's. In chapter 4, *Mastering the Art of French Cooking* by Julia Child, Louisette Bertholle, and Simone Beck gave me a wealth of information about the wonderful and talented Julia Child. In chapters 5 and 6, in addition to great books and other Internet sites, I used Leite's Culinaria, a great website with a piece titled "Dining Through the Decades" by David Leite to aid me in gathering together the reasons behind the changing food trends in the United States. In chapters 7 and 8, I found two articles, "A Saveur Roundtable: Ten Years of Cooking and Eating in America, 1994–2004" edited by Colman Andrews in *Saveur* magazine and "Freshening Up Fast Food" by Kim Severson in the *San Francisco Chronicle Magazine*, very helpful with their opinions about what the state of American food is today and how it could change in the future.

In addition to the above publications, I also visited COPIA: the American Center for Wine, Food, and the Arts in Napa, California, where I was able to view a fantastic exhibition called, Forks in the Road: Food, Wine and the American Table. I also had the pleasure of dining at Chez Panisse in Berkeley, California, on a delicious plate of bollito misto (grass-fed beef, chicken, and spring vegetables with horseradish salsa) and experiencing firsthand the fresh food served at this world-famous restaurant.

Bibliography

Anderson, Jean. *American Century Cookbook The Most Popular Recipes of the 20th Century*. New York: Clarkson N. Potter, 1997.

Andrews, Colman. "A Saveur Roundtable: Ten Years of Cooking and Eating in America, 1994–2004." *Saveur*, October 2004, 82–100.

Associated Press. Don Babwin. "A Truly Golden Anniversary for These Arches." *Modesto Bee*, April 15, 2005.

————. Juliana Barbassa. "Harvesting a Healthy Cash Crop." *Modesto Bee*, March 5, 2005.

————. Libby Quaid. "Out with the Old Pyramid, In with 12 New Ones." *Arizona Daily Sun*, April 20, 2005.

Beard, James. *Hors D'Oeuvre & Canapés*. Philadelphia: Running Press, 1940.

Bowers, Douglas E. "Cooking Trends Echo Changing Roles of Women." *Food Review*. January–April 2000. http://www.ers.usda.gov/publications/foodreview/jan2000/frjan20 (December 15, 2004).

Child, Julia, Louisette Bertholle, and Simone Beck. *Mastering the Art of French Cooking*. 40th anniversary ed. New York: Alfred A. Knopf, 2004.

Cunningham, Marion. *The Fannie Farmer Cookbook*. 13th ed. New York: Alfred A. Knopf, 2003.

Curran, Sally. "At the Two-Year Mark: Can You Still Trust the Organic Label?" *Vegetarian Times Magazine*, October 2004, 75–82.

Edwards, Owen. "Tray Bon! Thanksgiving Leftovers—260 Tons in All—Gave Birth to an Industry." *Smithsonian Magazine*. December 2004. http://www.smithsonianmag.si.edu/smithsonian/issues04/dec04/object.html (February 2005).

Harmon, John E. "The Better Burger Battle." *Atlas of Popular Culture in the Northeastern United States*. January 1997. http://www.geography.ccsu.edu/harmonj/atlas/burgers.html (February 19, 2005).

Hayes, Joanne Lamb. *Grandma's Wartime Kitchen*. New York: St. Martin's Press, 2000.

Hopkinson, Deborah. *Fannie in the Kitchen*. New York: Atheneum Books for Young Readers, 2001.

Leite, David. "Dining Through the Decades: Food of the 1920s, 1930s, 1940s, 1950s, 1960s, 1970s, 1980s, and 1990s. 1999." *Leite's Culinaria*. N.d. http://www.leitesculinaria.com/ features/dining4.html (January 29, 2005).

"Different Types of Vegetarians." *Living Vegetarian*. N.d. http://www.jtcwd.com/vegie/types.html (March 7, 2005).

McCutcheon, Marc. *Everyday Life from Prohibition Through World War II*. Cincinnati: Writer's Digest Books, 1995.

McGinn, Dan. "Insights: McDonald's Case Study: Burger Time." *MBA Jungle Magazine.* May 2001. http://www.mbajungle.com/magazine.cfm?INC=inc_article.cfm&ar (February 21, 2005).

Nickles, Harry G., and the editors of Time-Life Books. *Middle Eastern Cooking.* New York: Time-Life Books, 1969.

Rombauer, Irma S., and Marion Rombauer Becker. *Joy of Cooking.* New York: Bobbs-Merrill Company, Inc., 1975.

Severson, Kim. "Freshing Up Fast Food." *San Francisco Chronicle Magazine,* August 29, 2004, 10–15.

Smith, Andrew F. "Tacos, Enchiladas and Refried Beans: The Invention of Mexican-American Cookery." Address, Symposium, Oregon State University. 1999. http://food.oregonstate.edu/ref/culture/mexico_smith.html (September 25, 2004).

Smith, Jeff. *The Frugal Gourmet on Our Immigrant Ancestors.* New York: Avon Books, 1990.

Taco Bell. "Taco Bell Founder Glen Bell to Be Inducted into the Junior Achievement National Business Hall of Fame." News Release. April 25, 2001. http://www.tacobell.com/ourcompany/press/janbhf.htm (January 11, 2005).

Trager, James. *The Food Chronology.* New York: Henry Holt and Company, 1995.

Truelsen, Stewart. "TV Dinners: A Milestone in Food Marketing." *The Voice of Agriculture Views.* October 7, 2002. http://www.fb.org/views/focus/fo2002/fo1007.html (February 14, 2005).

Van Amber, Rita. *Stories and Recipes of the Great Depression of the 1930s.* Vol. 3. Neenah, WI: Van Amber Publishers, 1997.

Waters, Alice. *Chez Panisse Fruit.* New York: HarperCollins Publishers, 2002.

Index

Text copyright © 2007 by Loretta Frances Ichord
Illustrations copyright © 2007 by Jan Davey Ellis

Millbrook Press, Inc.
A division of Lerner Publishing Group
241 First Avenue North
Minneapolis, MN 55401 U.S.A.

Website address: www.lernerbooks.com

Library of Congress Cataloging-in-Publication Data

Ichord, Loretta Frances.
    Double cheeseburgers, quiche, and vegetarian burritos : American
cooking into the twenty-first century / by Loretta Frances Ichord ;
illustrated by Jan Davey Ellis.
        p.   cm. — (Cooking through time)
    Includes bibliographical references and index.
    ISBN-13: 978–0–8225–5969–6 (lib. bdg. : alk. paper)
    ISBN-10: 0–8225–5969–2 (lib. bdg. : alk. paper)
    1. Cookery, American—History—Juvenile literature. 2. Food habits—
United States—History—21st century—Juvenile literature. I. Ellis, Jan Davey.
II. Title. III. Series.
TX715.I223 2007
394.1'0973—dc22

                                        2005024535

Manufactured in the United States of America
1 2 3 4 5 6 – DP – 12 11 10 09 08 07